a complete work in progress

Nia   Mahmud

For Abuelita: the light you brought to this world made me who I am today. I miss you.

Te amo con todo mi corazon.

Content Warning

This collection contains some pieces relating/alluding to topics that might be sensitive to some readers, such as the following:

Mental health
Grief/Death
Gender based violence
Disordered eating

a complete work in progress

table of contents

Breaking

the art of breaking silently

Don't discuss complex emotions;
the things that are real.

Keep it bottled up.

Show strength,
resilience.

Whatever you do-

don't

        fall

                apart.

sugar overload

Chipped nails,
polish scratched off,
ripping at the chocolate's wrapper.
They say chocolate's good for the soul.
Well, let's see--
it's strewn atop the dresser
in haphazard piles--
she can't bring herself to stop.
Cheery pink aluminum
crumpled into a discarded heap at her side,
nearly toppling at its height.

Drowning in her emotions already, she figures--
what more is chocolate?
What more is a few wrappers?
Let them drown her.
Let her be lost beneath
raging blue-green waves.
Salt water and sea foam
swelling into bile,
mingling with words unsaid
and too little, too lates.
Pounding against her skull,
the room performing a dance routine,
putting her in a trance.

Either way, it doesn't matter-
brain splattered
on the too bright
white tile.
Swimming with vomit
that smells sweet, too sweet-
from the chocolate,
she supposes.

She will do what she wants
and no one will stop her.
Sticky hands
heart beating, faster, faster,
is in her control.
Not like everything else.

The sugary poison is the antidote.
Please, let it cleanse her
from the acid on her lips.
Let the chocolate wash everything else away.

valedictorian

They say she's got her head on straight,
she balances everything so great.
What they don't know
is that putting on a show is killing her.

Long nights declining all invites.
Studying instead, trying to get ahead
of the breakdown she knows is coming,
mind numbing.
Wondering if she's designed
to forever be confined,
forever suffocating under the weight
her facade creates.

She's scared of the way she falls apart,
wouldn't it break her parent's hearts
if they knew just how broken she was?
She thinks she has no reason to feel this way--
'just get through today,'
'it'll all be okay,'
'you are okay.'
Internal monologue gets her pretty far along
(infinitely more impressive than her grades
is how she puts herself back together
every single time.)

'Maybe if I try a little harder,
be a little smarter,
I won't feel this way.
I can't feel this way.'
What she doesn't know
is that keeping it up
when she can't anymore
(and she can't anymore)
will destroy her.

a tired mirror

They think she doesn't sleep well,
(can exhaustion last a lifetime?
Put you under a hazy spell?)
In reality she's wearied by the voices in her head
turning her subconscious into a battlefield of--
'you're not good enough,'
'just tough it up,'
'yes I will disrupt your day.'
'Do you think anyone believes your flimsy display?'

It's a fight to get out of bed.
Bones brittle,
cracking under the weight
of the hate they withstand.

Call it sleepless nights, heavy eyes, but
she can't fit this grief in her cupped hands.
It is a heavy weight that demands to be held,
pressing down on her chest.

Cupped hands, splashing water on her face.
Who is this girl in the mirror? Who is she?
The water doesn't wake her up,
it never does.

If her mind was
the grimy glass of a mirror
and her body, the wooden frame;
its cracks and fractures
wouldn't have to be a game
of "what would you rather call it today?"

The shattered mirror is broken,
she is only tired.
It is temporary, fixable:
this is what she tells the cracked glass.

it'll be morning soon

The sun blinds her, burns her.
It reminds her that everyone
looks at her like she does the sky —
squinting, thinking she is
too much and too bright.

Does everyone apply their words like sunscreen,
glances as glasses?
Why does the girl slather on the sunscreen
and wear the largest lenses herself?

'Do they seek the shade?' the sun asks. The girl asks.
Are they hiding from her? Can she join them?
Is there any hiding from yourself? From the sun?

It's a storm, these questions,
and who takes an umbrella to a hurricane?
Who answers the thunder and lighting
without fear of being struck?

The girl does.
She opens her eyes, stares into the storm
every time.

The sun cannot be struck by lightning,
so it is in these moments the girl is not the sun.
Not unbearable, not too bright.
It is in these moments one question
lingers on her lips.
'When does the storm end?
This storm is unbearable,
the sun is unbearable. How can I be both?'

impossible wishes

It's such bullshit to romanticize self-hate. It's a fight
every day, battling every thought.
You wish you wouldn't have to,
you wish it would end.
But that's an unreachable dream-
as impossible as fairies and mermaids.
Your heart buries these dreams
(all of them,)
for it is childish to wish for things
that can never be.

There is nothing romantic
about the panic that presses
on your shoulder blades,
razor sharp blades.
You like to switch between worries from yesterday
and worries for tomorrow;
letting them linger
like a lollipop
on your tongue.

There is nothing romantic
about the way you collapse,
unravel at the seams
like your favorite doll growing up.

Your back against the wall,
spine curved like the worm
that makes its way into your head.
It's an earworm singing songs
of inadequacy;
fanatically shaking your head-
'no no no,'
'I don't have to listen to you.'

There is nothing romantic
about the way you embrace the tears
that linger on your long eyelashes
like a wish;
a wish for tomorrow and no more of this.
You used to wish on shooting stars,
fallen stars.
Now you know
that those shooting stars
are nothing more than fallen soldiers,
forgotten by their brethren.

The sky is crying as you are crying-
that shooting star can't help you, dear.
It's hoping to be saved
just as much as you are-
and there's nothing romantic about it.

third person

Girl writes poems about herself in the third person.
She wonders if this makes her conceited.
Is it self-important to
compare yourself to a catastrophe
if it is more palatable that way?
(I want to learn to write about myself
in the first person.
What do I think of me? That has to matter.)

Girl doesn't know how to define herself
if not in metaphors,
if not in the shape of something else.
Girl is a valedictorian, a poisoned ivy, a paper straw -
    what more could she be?

She doesn't recognize her own reflection;
only catches glimpses
in everyone else's fun house, carnival mirrors.
(I recognize that stretched out version of me,
the too tall version,
it's the mirror someone else showed me.)
Girl is a city, a mirror, a zombie.
(What more can I be?)
It isn't meant to be palatable for readers,
(it's for me.)

She can see beauty in metaphors
but is still learning to find beauty in herself.
If she compares herself to something else—
maybe she'll find someone worth writing about.

i'm fine

Yeah,
I'm fine.
Each rapid breath
inhaling knives.
The gaping holes in my stomach are
nothing compared to the storms in my head.

Each tear
streaming down my face
is liquid fire,
burning me up.
Leaving streaks upon my cheeks;
nothing compared to the scalding self-hatred
that resides in every part of me.

Each guttural sob
sounds like I've been gutted.
Or maybe it's a wild animal,
anxious to tear me apart.
But I've already torn myself apart.
A mix match-
assortment of bones,
organs,
and blood
that don't quite go together
when dismembered
and put back together.

Really,
there's no need to worry-
I'm fine.

I have to be.

the unseen

The darkness behind my eyelids
is comforting.
Luring me
to a place where I don't have to feel.
(I mustn't submit.)

i'll do it tomorrow

Remember that day a car sped by?
I was almost run over and I said that
I didn't have time for it,
there was no room in my schedule for
a hospital visit.
It's just how it happens sometimes, isn't it?
Death knocked on frosty windows
and I waved away the feathery black wings,
waved off the scythe glinting in the moonlight.

I said, 'come back at the same time tomorrow,
and then you can take me.
I have a test in the morning, you see:
an important meeting, a project to present.'

After that- I'll open the window
and hold Death's hand.
I'll be ready to pull on a coat and skate
on the river Lethe.
After that, nothing.
After that, I won't remember the test I took,
the busy day I made Death wait for,
but at least I've finished everything
worth doing on earth.

I asked Death to pity me; my wish was granted--
I asked Life to have mercy; it could not do the same.

i was never good at gardening

I couldn't tell you what's wrong.
I only know
that all I look forward to after waking up
is going to sleep again.
The things that once made me happy
now leave a dull ache
in the place where my heart used to grin.

Trying to write results in blank staring
at an equally blank screen.
Reading feels like poking my brain
with hot rods.
Speaking with friends
feels like someone's twisting my insides
and tearing them out of my body
(again and again).

This is me: overfilling every cup,
this is the emptiness that follows it.
I've given everyone else the love,
patience,
respect,
and compassion I needed.
I learned to become what everyone else
wanted me to be. This is me: overfilling
on love for everyone else's garden while
drowning in contempt for my own.

Nothing I do is enough, it's never enough and
I could spend the rest of my life trying
to come to terms with that.

Don't tell me that the grass isn't greener
on the other side-
it is, I know it is.
I'm the one that gave it the water to thrive.

the allure of dreaming

The soft rays of sunshine
slipping through the cracks in my blinds
urge me into waking.
They hold promises of a bright day
(an empty assurance I'm used to).

I close my eyes briefly
but tightly,
as if the dancing dots that appear
can transport me back to dreamland.

Fantastical, delusional, everything-is-better land.
Visions spun from cotton candy clouds-
dancing around the pitfalls in my personality,
listening instead to songs preaching individuality.
(There's something special
in my character, apparently.)

Tip-toeing past the landmines of my temper,
wouldn't want to tempt her-
the writhing, sleepy monster that lies there.
Jumping over the ditch that holds
my discarded aspirations,
it's best not to focus on my limitations-
once I fall in, I won't be able to find my way out.

Even in sleep, I'm unwelcome in a perfect reality.
Seldom can I imagine
anything but hiding from myself.
I could never recognize a good thing,
I could never want a good thing.

Even in my dreams it seems
I can't escape from me.

i only watch reruns

I paint everything as a tragedy,
(even when it isn't; especially when it isn't).
Every mile of distance between me
and everyone I've ever loved
is a somber song echoing
in the chambers of my mind.
And it is a chamber
or perhaps it's a cage.
A place where I rewatch the history
of every person that no longer thinks of me.

I see everything through a discolored lens.
Every beginning disguised as an inevitable ending,
every glimmer of dawn is one second closer
to dusk.

Everything changes, everything is different now-
but I am still the same.
Mourning every moment that has ended-
every show on its final season,
every season of change
where I remain stagnant.

I don't see how this world
can be anything but tragic.

when nature mourned with me

Every time I said goodbye-
I held your hand, smiled and
told you I loved you
like it would be the last time.

None of it could prepare me
for when it really was the last time.

I tried to soften the blow;
but losing you could be nothing less
than the wind blowing through the trees,
howling in the dark night
with uncertainty. Everything is uncertain
without you.

Animals burrowing deeper into their holes,
flowers wilting,
the sun faltering.

Most days I wonder how the earth kept spinning.
Most days nature is left mourning you too.

exile

I am exiled with the wave of a hand,
irrelevant on a whim.
I am banished with one slamming door,
made small with the screams.

The door's slam echoes against the wall,
echoes in my head.
The screams and shouts drown out any little voice
within me that sometimes tells me
I'm good enough.
Only on occasion, only on the holidays
where I am not exiled.
Now there is no one to tell me I am good enough.
If not myself, who?
Who would tell me such a thing?

This is love, this is love, this is love.
There is so much writing about what love is
and I am no exception. What a concept,
what a figment of imagination.

This exile is lonely but I'm not sure I know how
to live with anything else.

I'll tell you what love is: a learned behavior.

Love is banishment, loud voices, slamming doors.
It is an exile from one's good graces.
It is the exemptions,
conditions to their adoration.

poison ivy

"I'm sorry," I say, before running away.
I'm convinced these toxins are contagious;
a rapidly spreading rash
of poison ivy lives in my head.

I am not girl-
made of sugar and spice and all things nice.
I am toxic waste
made of glowing bacteria
from the nuclear plant's backyard.
The shattered tv left on the road,
shards rearranged to resemble a heart.
I am an old car battery,
and engine exhaust is the air I breathe.

I am not cinnamon buns and warm lattes,
sunny days or sweet like honey.
I am sharp edges and rotting fruit,
rain clouds and breakdowns.

No one ever asks the poison ivy
how it feels being hard to love.
How it feels to accidentally suffocate
that which you love.
To be a weed you pull and toss aside,
watching flowers become bouquets
handed to lovers like a gift.

I leave rashes on calloused hands
and everyone hates me for it.
I hate me for it.

when i belonged to the fog

Spinning, falling, it was all dizzying.
Who was there? How long did it last?
A day, a week, a month?
Heavy mist hangs over the mind;
I call it my friend.

But here's what I remember:
fear; suffocating and loud,
so loud. A roaring in my ears
told me that it would never end:
that day, the memory of it.

I remember the earth halting on its axis,
me in the aftermath. Terrible things
happen every day but it seemed
I was the only one who could not
forget it. One person's world ends and
everyone else moves on. Not me.

I remember that grief so well
it stings my skin. I could not help her,
no one else could-
how could that be?
I'm sorry. I'm so sorry.

Before the fog settled, there was
a voice. Many voices.
'You aren't safe here, you aren't safe
anywhere. You do not belong to
yourself. You belong to the fog.'
 I'm sorry, I'm so sorry,
I wish my sorries could change everything.

I don't know why it never left-
this fear, this anger, this guilt.
I always knew the symptoms of
womanhood. I always knew that I would
spend my whole life hiding from violence.
I shouldn't have to. You shouldn't have had to.
I'm sorry, I'm so sorry.

The mist is suffocating, it is liberating;
the voices can't make it through.

laughter isn't always the best medicine

One day my discomfort
won't be a punchline
in my own joke.

A stand-up comedy routine
meant to mask
a reality I'd rather not live in.

the birds know more than me

All the birds are singing a song but
I don't know the melody
so suddenly I'm drowning in it.
Their little song, this life.
The lyrics I came up with on my own
might be wrong;
I don't sing them. I could never
sound as pretty anyways.
I'd never measure up to those birds
and their perfect songs.

They're chirping but it sounds more
like a relentless laughing,
wheezing, teasing the girl who tries
to learn their songs.
The girl who decides on that particular day the birds
and their day-to-day life is the most important thing
that has ever existed.

Isn't it? I wake up and you're singing,
I go to sleep and you're singing
and I can't be alive one more second not knowing
what's so great that you're always singing?
What's so great?
What's worth your endless song,
the melody I cannot memorize?
Tell me, little bird, what makes you so happy
you have to scream about it?
From the tops of trees, from rooftops,
from above the clouds?

What you have, I want. Tell me your song, please.
Tease me all you want,
but tell me what it is that's so special
it deserves all the trouble.
Tell me what you see in this life; give me your song.

a lifetime

They say it takes about twenty-one days
to form a habit,
but it only took one look in the mirror
to begin berating the reflection staring back.
One cut on the sharp edge of my thoughts
to begin adding band-aids to the grocery list.

It only took one day of unhappiness
to convince myself that I would always feel its grip.

They say it takes about three days to break a habit,
but what if this is all I know?

What if it takes a lifetime?

i want it all and i hate it

I'm skating on thin ice
but I've never been brave enough to
jump into a frozen lake. Skidding, slipping,
never letting the floor beneath me give out.
The ground always feels like it's going to disappear
from underneath me
so I do everything I can not to let it.

I'm not brave enough to
                    jump into
                            a frozen lake.

I'm not brave enough to make the ice break
because I've seen what happens when it does.
When it shatters, I do too.

I'm watching the sun rise;
refusing to become Icarus.
Watching trees grow;
refusing to climb them.

I've stopped believing the ice won't freeze me,
the sun won't burn me, the horizon won't scold me.
I'm always thinking of the aftermath,
the moments following.

Jumping in the lake
and becoming the sun
and marveling at the horizon
sounds fun.
But if I did that,
I would never stop wanting more.

everyone hates paper straws

You don't like paper straws, you tell me.
They aren't any good for slurping milkshakes
and they fall apart in your hand.

You do like me, you say,
but that's only because you think I'm a plastic straw.
You think that I can hold it all together,
that I am resilient.
Even if you put me in the garbage
or threw me out to sea,
I would live for centuries.

None of this is true,
and I don't know how I got you to believe it.

In reality, I am a paper straw.
I am flaky, weak,
will fall apart again and again.
I'm no good at slurping milkshakes:
sometimes I'll cry at cookies and cream
for no reason at all.

When you tell me what an inconvenience
these paper straws are, I'll agree:
"I don't blame you for disliking paper straws.
I don't like them either."

I don't know how to tell you
that you're sitting across from one.

car crash

If a luxury car has a few scratches,
do you throw it out? Fix it? Love it?
I'm wondering when I became a car at all.
When did I become something to fix?

My engine burns out quicker than I'd like to admit;
always refueling
and never full.

I don't know how to slow down.
I only know how to be the wreckage, the aftermath;
crashing and burning,
swerving out of control,
the wheel jolting in my hands.

Normally I am out of control,
somewhere between hating it
and not knowing anything else.

One day I will love my scratches;
they won't be something to repair or paint over.
One day I'll obey the speed limit;
cruise instead of collide.
One day I'll hold the steering wheel
and forge my own lane.

One day my growth won't
be measured by metaphors.

It will be real.

Mahmud

Discovering

on the subway home

I realize I don't know where home is
while gripping to grimy plastic seats,
gripping to dreams with both hands.
I'm coming home from something-
I don't know where I was or where I'm going.

If I find a home in the journey;
the sticky subway floor
with cheery pink wrappers
scattered like discarded dreams,
then maybe I should make a bed
across the dull gray seats.
I should use a blanket made of stories,
woven from the whispers
of passerby along for the ride.

If I could just make a home on the subway,
it would be easier to see that nobody in the seats
or clinging to the handrails
knows where they're going either.

They stumble on and off the subway-
convinced it will get them where they need to go.
And maybe it will.
But it is not a question of 'where they need to go,'
but rather 'where they want to go.'
It's easy to stumble into a day and a life
and a string of choices;
forgetting that wanting was ever there at all.

I want to recognize the joy of the journey
and not the emptiness of where I've ended up.

your game; my life

You saunter over
with your easy grin
and easy laugh.
All smiles, all teeth,
walking towards me with
everything else that is so easy for you
about being here, about being anywhere.

I sit with my jaw clenched,
nails dug deep into skin.
I hold my screams, hold my breath.
Sometimes I've got this urge to
stand up, shout obscenities, flip
the board. Take your king.
Then you'd be the one cowering,
retreating into yourself
like the spectacle you've turned me into.

How can you not see
what you do to me?

I won't be quiet so you can be comfortable.
I'll scream until
glass shatters;
just as you shattered me

over
and over.
I'll jump until
the floorboards
tremble and give out,
force you to tumble
and fall
all the way down;
till you've made it to hell.
Then maybe you'll see
what you make earth for me.

Stop, stare, and point at the way
you fall. At the way no one offers
a hand. There's always more time to sink-
you made sure of it. Spinning and falling-
you would be the spectacle. You would lose.

Or maybe I'll just sit here.
Play by your rules, lose my king,
lose everything.
Teeth clenched,
cracking.
Picture perfect smile,
silent.

There is no winning in a game
designed with you as the winner.
I can imagine victory all I want,
the roles reversed. At the end:
it's your game
but my life.

birthright

Someday these screams building
with the bile in my throat
will find a way out.
I have held them there for generations.
Inherited this building
shriek from my mother, and her mother before her.
My brother inherits a watch,
I inherit screams that never stop.

Nothing belongs to me--
not this body, not this life, not this continent--
but this birthright is mine.

wanting a clean slate

"Where did you go?"
I'm asked when I get that vacant look in my eyes.
I wish I could be more like the blank piece of paper
that my eyes resemble in these moments.
I wish I wasn't littered with scribbles,
crumpled and ripped all over.

In those moments my mind is anything but blank,
anything but a pristine sheet of copy paper.
I'm reliving times that I'd rather not remember.
I'm taken back to hands shaking,
heart breaking, stomach aching-
it feels so real.
Playing on a loop in my mind-
writing and crossing it out,
writing and crossing it out.

I can never seem to erase it completely.

i am always haunted or haunting

When I finally wandered through the house
you had lived in,
I tried to convince myself it was just that-
a house-
not a home
housing all the memories I would give everything
to live in again.

It was impossible.
I saw a ghost in your room-
my cries echoing against the walls
and reverberating in the emptiness.
I was transported to your last days-
I could reach out and touch the oxygen machine
that helped you breathe,
hear the tv rattle mindlessly.
I could see you smiling, bright,
like you had all the time in the world left.

Your hospital bed that had given the room
such dreary undertones
was back in its spot.
I hated that bed, what it meant.
I wish you could know
that I don't remember you that way.

I remember you taking me through your garden,
hearing your stories at the kitchen table,
baking you a cake for your birthday.
But here's the ghost, your ghost, asking me
about my memories.

Here is your ghost, reaching out for my hand.
I always held your hand like it was fragile,
when really it felt so strong-
like you would live forever.
But I knew you wouldn't, and you didn't-
because you're gone now.

The room is empty,
stripped of any trace of you.
All that's left is me and the space
my memories alone cannot fill.

me: pleading with soil

This longing is nothing more than closing my eyes
and shaking my fist at the sky. I am suffocating
on this longing, it's lodged in my throat with
whispered words of ancestors I can't reach
(I can't reach them, I can't reach them,
they don't know me.)

How am I supposed to belong to a place
I've never truly known? How will they love me?

It is more than a continent separating us. More than
an ocean. More than something a plane can cross.
If I step foot on your soil and you reject me-
if you call me a stranger, say it's been too much time-
what then? Then, I would take the longing in a
heartbeat, the not knowing.

I would rather imagine you love me
than know you never could.

I'm pleading with soil, crawling on hands and knees
towards a home that does not recognize me.

what i mean

Words are not enough to save me. And by this
I mean
writing is not enough, poetry is not enough
to have anything make sense.
And by this I mean
I'm tired of always having to explain 'what I mean.'
Because I am a bumbling catastrophe.
Juggling words like party tricks
that lose the appeal once everyone knows
how it works.
I mean I am teetering on the edge of oblivion
because how can anything be real if it doesn't
make sense? If I can't explain it?

Maybe it's destiny; this spine pulling,
chest crushing, windpipe bursting
catastrophe I call life.
Maybe poetry isn't enough to save me.
Maybe nothing is.

rainy days

Dew drops and rain plops,
bright blue dress,
soaking wet.

You love the weather however it chooses to come-
finding muses peeking out at you-
hiding in leaking foliage from above.

Flickering street lights
illuminate the joy on your face.
You're a siren,
calling to those
cozy and comfortable
within their busy brick homes.
Fireplaces roaring,
revoking your calls
pleas, really:
to let go,
to dance in the rain.

They peer at your silhouette
from their dusty rectangular windows.
You're tainted in vignette:
any artist would've been so happy.
Raindrops racing down the grimy glass,

thundering sky above,
dreary monochrome,
and then you-
a bright and bustling soul in the middle of it all.
You're simply angelic
with a pull that's absolutely magnetic.
But these figurines in their neat-freak,
stripped-clean houses
see you as nothing more than a threat.
There are no artists here.

You couldn't care less
about their silly stares
and tedious talking.
You're having too much fun
leaping into puddles,
smearing dirt on your face.

Really, they wish to join you-
and they would if only
there wouldn't be more important things going on-
death and taxes,
lingering on their last breath,
artificial happiness for the masses.

august

August is me: standing on the precipice of summer
and whatever comes after.
I've never known what happens
when it's over, I never really wanted to.
I'm still living in the summers of my childhood;
still sitting at the bottom of pools,
closing my eyes, holding my breath.

This August I sat at my friend's kitchen counter
and watched her prepare lunch for the next day.
I drank my water and tapped my feet, thinking:
she would be here tomorrow with
the same routine.
The same frenzied movements, the same dance.
There are no guarantees for next month or next year;
she might be here next to me,
she might be in her dream city.

August will end and I don't want to see
what comes next.
I remember when youth was forever,
when it stretched farther
than magical in-betweens of preparing meals,
preparing our hearts for all the ways we would
fall apart.

I remember when we used to wish for rain
so we could play Monopoly for longer;
and so later, we could
ride our bikes through the puddles.
I remember when we both held on to summer
with both hands. When did you let go?
When did I?

When fall arrives, please
look me in the eyes and tell me
August will come again next year.
Tell me it's not over forever.
Tell me I can still dwell in pools,
in kitchens, in rain puddles.

Tell me there's still a place for me here.

fine print

Growing up comes with growing pains,
childhood nothing more than link chains
holding us back from something more.
We're told we've no clue what's in store-
while we still can we should explore
before stepping out that new door.
Throw away what you once adored-
hide your memories in the drawer
with knives that are hard to ignore.
Both equally dangerous you're
aware the threats that drawer contains-
beware of the youth in your veins.

conversation starters

I want to talk about the way
a year sounds when it flies over my shoulders,
how it moves too quickly to catch or to hold onto.
The way irony feels against my skin-
red welt, impact- it sends me flying.
I want to talk about how a burst of inspiration tastes,
sweet with certainty and undertones of success.

I want to talk about the rough surface
of anxiety I try to soothe,
prickly against my pink palm.

Everyone else just wants to talk about the weather.
Not about how the thundering sky might be sad,
but, *how inconvenient that is for us.*

photo albums

Faded photo strips
smell of dusk and bags of chips.
Nights we spent dancing in the surf,
the moon hanging over our heads
like a promise of tomorrow and always.

It feels like the warm embrace
of campfires; we made smores with
the tangible remains of our laughter.

I couldn't tell you
when the pictures started to fade.
If we no longer have our youth
and what we were once so convinced
meant everything,
what do we have?

why i'm not good at chemistry

We had chemistry,
so it's a shame we're strangers now.
Because when we weren't it was sparks flying,
silly remarks and gravity defying.
In our own little bubble floating above the ground,
we tripped in rubble on the way back down.

I've since learned a thing or two about chemistry.
It was foolish to think our chemistry
meant permanence-
that it meant longevity
or love.
We were only ever two opposite elements-
take and give,
act and react-
I was always the one giving and reacting.

I don't know much about chemistry
in the practical sense. I knew your bright smiles
that rivaled the stars. I knew what you loved
and I knew that sometimes it included me.
I knew you. I didn't know myself.

I'm never going to be good at chemistry
or forever if I don't know what to do
with my reflection.

starry skies, starry eyes

There are stars in your eyes.
Now, in the darkness of night;
you see me as an angel
that fell from the very sky
we gaze at.
My laugh holds some sort of magic,
like a fairy flapping their wings.
My voice sounds like a promise
of forever.
But what happens
when that same sky
brightens with the sun
and a new day?
When the stars fade from the sky,
will the stars in your eyes
disappear?

never fall in love with a poet

When you fall in love with a poet,
they will turn your smile
into the sun.
Murky brown eyes
into burning embers.
You will be nothing more than a metaphor.

I wish I didn't see smiles as galaxies
or eyes as fires.
I wish I could see people as they are.
Love their crooked smiles, love their dull eyes.
I shouldn't turn it into something beautiful
when it's not.

Never fall in love with a poet
because I will romanticize your heartbreak
as I romanticize my own.
Your heart torn in two
is suddenly the sky falling
and mountains moving.
Your tears become oceans
and unrelenting rain.

People are not poems
or the metaphors I use
to understand the world.

If people are not poems,
they are just that-
human.
They don't exist as metaphors
and ideals- they are real.

If people are not poems,
I don't know how to love them.

last forever

If this isn't going to last forever,
let's hang up paintings as if there is a
tomorrow in which we sit, drink our morning coffee,
and stare at art.
Let's move the furniture around as if we will
watch TV from the couch's new position,
eat dinner from where the dining table now sits.

Argue with me as if tomorrow,
there will be resolutions.
So for today, we'll scream at nothing.
I want to go outside and dance in the rain,
complaining about getting sick like we have time
to get there.

If this isn't going to last forever,
please just let me pretend that it will.

my eyes on you, never on the road

I wasn't blindsided. I could see our ending
coming from a mile away.
But I barreled forward anyways.
I stepped on the gas regardless.

When it comes to us,
                              the only ending is-

Me: hurtling off a cliff.
You: looking on curiously.

I braced for impact, crashed, sat in the chasm
you created. I watched you smile,
you watched me catch fire.

We were a book of matches:
our story could only end in flames.

the climb to the top

One day I won't whisper your name
in the cracks and dips within my poetry.
One day I will shout it from the top of the canyon-
it will float away with the breeze-
its significance lost on me.

making permanent homes in temporary times

Suffocating silence turns into breathless laughter,
2000s playlist on shuffle,
last minute plans on borrowed time.
Blinding neon lights-
closer, closer-
across the globe.
Friends turned into family or something more-
it's a family chosen.
It's "you can leave, but will not,"
staying through the three am breakdowns,
dark car rides.
Rather than holding my hand through the dark,
they give me the power to light my own way again.

There isn't a choice to stay when it gets hard,
no split-second hesitation-
staying is as certain as a steady heartbeat,
sure as the spidery veins tracing the path to my heart.
There's no choice, no way to rip out a part of myself
and remain whole.

It terrifies me-
loving in full measures,
not having a choice to leave the people
who have made home in my heart.
It terrifies me- playlists, plans, proximity, distance-
it all ends. It all ends and is forgotten
but I'm still here,
I always am. It terrifies me
because more people have made home in my heart
than I have in theirs.

when the ocean is hard to find

When the ocean is hard to find,
I locate the north star-
not because it will lead me to the sea-
but because it's something I know with certainty.

I've grown up on the ocean's shores,
water lapping to my knees.
Where has it gone?
What does it mean when I can't see it?

If the ocean covers most of the earth
and I can't find it,
where am I?
If I can't see the ocean,
does that mean it isn't there?
If the people I care about fade into the horizon,
does that mean that they no longer care?

What if I am alone?
What if I leave this earth and
it remembers nothing of me?
What if the very ocean I'm searching for
washes away my footprints?
My ashes?

Stop. Breathe.

Look for the north star.
Isn't that enough?
There is at least one constant,
one thing that won't change.
Isn't that enough?

Why is it never enough?

warning: fragile goods

I thought love was a beautifully packaged box.
I held my heart in my hands
like a present that would never need a gift receipt.

When, really, it is as gentle and soft
as a delivery truck tossing my heart out the window-
ignoring the sticker declaring 'fragile goods'.

Love was a mistaken address,
tape-tearing,
messing up, failing.

I cradled my heart in my hands,
passed it on to razor sharp claws,
and had it returned within thirty days.
It came back to me a little more broken
with shipping and handling
than it was before.

the dos and don'ts of moving on

Don't look back, don't look back-
I'm only looking forward now.
Forward, towards this lone
cracked cobblestone road.
Forward, the way I asserted
I don't want that anymore.
(I don't want it anymore. I don't, I don't.)

Looking down at the ground, at the loose asphalt
I had been so accustomed to falling in.
But the scrapes and bruises have healed-
there's no need to look back.

Looking up, at every star that now seems within
my reach. Up, towards the flickering lamp lights
that are guiding me towards a foreign place.
Foreign. Unknown. Looming.

I look back.

I see familiarity. I see crowded streets. Solid ground.
Empty skies. Steady light.
I see everything I've built.
I see memories I could live in
if I would just turn back.

But I won't.
 I won't turn back to live in a place I've outgrown.
Just because I built myself off the past,
doesn't mean I need to live in it.
It doesn't mean I need to want it.
I'm walking away from everything I built,
I'm leaving it there.

i am selfish

To be selfish is
an act of self-care.
It's a mercy; a peace treaty to myself.

In a world where I am selfish,
I look in the mirror
and pay my reflection a compliment.
It isn't taxing, I don't empty my pockets
for self-acceptance that comes naturally.

I demand a love that is good,
a love that holds my hands
without crushing my bones.

In a world where I am selfish,
I believe I am worth respect and
leave teeth marks on the hands
that tell me otherwise.

I'm sure of everything now.
I might change my mind tomorrow,
but on the days I don't apologize
for knowing my worth, I dance.

(Maybe there's nothing selfish about any of it.)

increasing city infrastructure funding

I am a city:
blinding lights, buildings, and all.
I hide notions of loneliness
under morning coffee and bustling streets.
I am surrounded by people and always alone.
I am back alleys and cracked cobblestone,
the layers of pollution;
concealer that doesn't mask my tired eyes.

In the city that is me,
rent is always free.
The loftiest condos and largest mansions
boast unlimited stay and amenities for passersby.
I stay in a shack at the city's end,
looking in on the daily happenings.
I watch the people, as if through
a foggy window.
They hug and kiss on subways,
they cry and dance through the streets.
When the days become too heavy to carry,
they have a hand to hold instead.

I want to join in. I want to be at the center of it all
instead of watching from the sidelines.

I'm kicking everyone out-
eviction notices mass mailed-
an exodus from the city that needs sleep.

I'm renovating before I allow anyone else inside.
Getting lost on my subways,
wandering the streets I haven't seen.
Making my own coffee; steam licking the cup's edge,
jumping in the puddles of murky rainwater.
I'm watching sunrises from the tallest skyscrapers,
holding the horizon's promise of new possibilities
in my hands.

It was easy to lose myself in the noise,
the stomping feet, the rough hands.
I couldn't realize how beautiful this life is
without stopping to look at, stopping to
make it mine.

Being

a world without pollution

Letting go of something
that was doomed from the start
was like breathing air
that wasn't polluted for the first time.

It was a forest of lush green
blooming in my lungs
where my existence had only ever been stifled.

I can't go back to anything else.

conversations with my mirror

I believe in small mercies like brushing my hair
when it's wet and not wishing it looked different.
I wash the sheets and sleep while it's still warm.
I dance around the kitchen to the music I grew up
listening to.

That's all life is. Handing out kindness
on street corners and hoping it sticks, but forgetting
to leave any for yourself. What I'm trying to say is
don't you see I'm always spinning with
my eyes closed and hiding the scrapes on my knees
from when I fall.

I believe in the
small mercy of accepting
a band-aid. Of leaving a little bit
of kindness for myself.

I don't always remember to smile at my reflection
but when I do I make a celebration of it. I put
ointment on my body and heal
everything the day has done.

it was always me

Your words eased the raging storm within me.
I finally felt as though
I
was
enough.
It was foolish for me to think
it had anything to do with you,
and not
everything to do with me.

my heart's mannerisms

I have convinced my heart of the beauty
in every passing day.
In the most obscure,
unlovable things.

I have urged my heart to love
even when it has seemed impossible.
Even when a love rattled my bones-
when the rib cage that housed my heart
feared it would collapse in on itself-
I still found some sort of wonder in the way
it nearly broke completely,
but refused to stop loving.
Even when I knew it would tear me apart
again,
and again,
and again.

As long as my heart beats
it will continue to fall in love
with everything it comes across.
I am learning to love this, too

love without restraints

I love you
is a phrase I used to think
was thrown around too casually,
too flippantly.
I used to hold my I love yous under my tongue
where no one could hear them.

I see, now, how wrong I was.

I see how the seasons greet every new dawn,
how the winds of change meet me in the middle.
My capacity for love used to feel mortifying,
now it's sunshine lifting me up.

I don't know much, but one thing I know for certain
is that I must let love grow without restraints.
It will grow with the weeds and the flowers,
dance in April showers.

I love you, I love you, I love you-
it doesn't sound like an apology anymore.

starry eyes turn to morning

Maybe I could have drawn it out,
not marveled at the constellations.
Maybe if I hadn't pointed out the beautiful things
you wouldn't have been reminded
that I'm not one of them.

The sky brightening used to devastate me.
I used to say:
I would do anything
for you to look at me like that again.
I would do anything to know what to do with it.

Now it doesn't matter, now I look at the sky
and see my reflection in the stars.

Now I say:

I will not be treated like a shooting star
when I am nothing less
than the whole universe.

a force of nature

Someone's lack of respect for me
does not equate to
not respecting myself.

Ask a hurricane what happens
when someone disregards their strength.
(It never ends well.)

The velocity of my winds
will demolish any foolish notions of power.
I am a storm inside of a girl,
and the only devastation
is to sentiments of self-importance.

games of ping pong

To be your friend was much different than
admiring the way your smile came,
put me in a daze more than the bright sun
(which burned and dizzied as we played ping-pong)
could hope to manage. The sun never made
my heart stutter in my chest or hands shake.

A lens had shifted suddenly, quickly,
the enormity of how lucky we
were to have met soon became a heavy
weight on my shoulders. I knew this game of
ping-pong was as short lived as this short week.

I didn't want only temporary,
fleeting memories, or laughs, or smiles.

I found myself wishing you were more like
the dull sun: for the sun is permanent,
and I so wished that we could be as well.

silence

If I went back, I'm sure everything would look
just as I left it. Heels by the door, scars on my feet.
Stars dazzling, promising a future we would
never see.

The traffic stilled in our wake. Everything halted.
I always thought we were that important-
we weren't. If I went back, I'd see the stillness
consume us. That's it. One last scowl,
one last glare. I left and the scars on my feet
healed.

I had nothing left to say to you, in the end.
Even if I did go back, I don't think I could fill
that suffocating silence.

(I don't know if I'd want to.)

power suits

The click-clacking
of those uncomfortable heels you wear
(but they feel powerful too, don't they?)
form a beat,
a rumbling of this scrubbed-white tile.
It reverberates all the way to
that boys club you weren't invited to.
The sound of your heels smacking the ground
creates an anthem.
It's heard by all girls that wear power suits.
It says 'you are not alone,'
'your voice is heard.'

When the clacking of your heels
syncs up with the unfamiliar girl next to you-
it's more than a coincidence-
it's a force of nature.

The synchronized,
almost musical sound
of your heels on the floor
at the same time as hers
is some sort of magic.

balancing act

Traveling with only the clothes on their backs
and a crying sister.
Native tongues in their mouths
that whisper and dream of a brighter future.
One family blending in
and standing out from the crowds.

Molding, transforming themselves,
a mixture of all they left behind
and all they hope to become.
Performing endless shows of conformity,
they train their tongues when they're called scum.
Scribbling their dreams in the margins
when it used to be the body paragraph.

But no, to make their dreams come true
is not to forget where they came from.
So they will barrel through the streets-
blasting the radios, banging on drums.

It is a game of give and take.
Giving up the home they once had,
but keeping their heritage alive.
Some days they win,
some days they are left tumbling down,
but every day is worth it.

zombie within you

When you're buried alive
you lose the drive
to simply survive.
You welcome the dirt shoveled over your nose,
stuck in between your toes,
it's like you can't wait to decompose.
(When you live with one foot in the grave
being buried is hardly a change.)

Nine to five,
when was the last time you wanted to be alive?
You denied yourself a life;
you're not meant to live solely with strife.
Doing what everyone else says
is "supposed" to make you happy,
but it doesn't.

You can't seem to shake this childish dream
that there has to be more than this.
It's a recurring theme, a lesson learned again
and again-
we were all happier years ago when we
didn't know what it all meant.

I hope one morning you'll wake up,
pour yourself a big ol' cup of coffee,
and dump it out onto your driveaway-
measure the precise way
to lose it completely-
it's only when you lose it
that you can really find anything,
especially yourself.
Smash that mug on the ground!
Yes, you're unwound!
But you've finally conquered
the zombie within you.

let's go on an adventure

When I say
'let's go for an adventure'
what I mean is:
Let's leave this party-
pulsing with neon lights and booming music,
let's play cards in the empty buffet.
Opaque granite table top the only testament
to our howling laughter
or who won which game.

When I whisper to you in the dead of night,
the darkness luring your tired eyes to sleep,
it almost seems like a dream:
'Let's stay up and watch the sunrise on the roof.'

What I mean is let's get lost
on this college campus.
Delirious with laughter
as we stumble through the streets-
not our streets but they might as well be-
there's no difference between
the cracks in the sidewalk
and my grin
when I try to understand the joke you made.

My laugh erodes lines onto my face,
the road we walk is long and winding
just like the punchline.
We are the same no matter where we go,
the city is a backdrop for our story,
never the other way around.

When we drive with your windows down
and I'm not in the passenger seat
but still in control of the aux,
I'll sing at the top of my lungs,
soundwaves lost on the cars zooming past.
We'll go to that fast food restaurant
that's open twenty-four hours.

What I mean is-
if we're together,
and we're laughing,
hearts overflowing-
that's all the adventure I need.

some things never change

Sticky summer sweat,
nights with no regrets.
Skipping to an unheard song-
staying out 'til dawn,
fighting off our yawns-
we are right where we belong.

These memories could
never be replaced.
This pink plastic slide has heard
our secret spilling,
grilling for details,
privy to all that's occurred.

Our lives didn't stretch
further than our pledge
to always remain best friends.
We would touch the sky
by swinging so high,
in parks we spent all our time.

Having silly fights
over our bug bites,
always resolved with brownies
and a game of tag,
winner gets to brag.
(How these times changed so quickly.)

Now we venture to
this park where we grew
for the nostalgia of it.
There are new secrets to spill,
and if we stand still-
those memories can still fit.

late night laundry and last minute road trips

Throwing my socks at you like a snowball fight-
competing to see who can fold clothes faster-
we are the only ones on this earth tonight.

Our lives are planned for us, encased in plaster-
this small deviation is temporary-
real recklessness would be a true disaster.

But right now, adventure feels necessary.
Your long laugh and glittering eyes makes it so:
let's go abandon the itinerary.

My heart could overflow, I'm ready to go.
Clothes on my back warm and fresh from the dryer-
I don't want to outgrow these last minute trips.

We have the entire world before us,
and I don't have any desire to quit.

at least someone is

Somewhere,
two teenagers are falling in love
under the twinkling stars.
Frolicking in a dreamy field
that smells of lavender and earth,
and things that are good and right.

Somewhere,
there is a bumbling little girl
who's just learned to read.
Stumbling around an old book shop that
shines in the sunlight
that's streaming in through the windows.
The crinkling papers
and the smell of ancient books
feels like home.

Somewhere,
there is an aspiring artist
who's just found her muse among the crowds.
Baby hairs sticking to the nape of her neck,
she's hurrying home to her paintbrush.

I wish I could be falling in love
in a field at dusk.
Or in awe of an old bookstore,
knowing it's where I belong.
Or in a crowd of people,
small, overjoyed by the wonder
and enormity of it all.

Maybe I'm not happy where I am right now,
but at least someone is.
And that has to count for something
right?

living in my memories

Flickering light bulbs look like whispers in the dark.
When I see a car speeding by,
I can hear music floating from its open windows,
screeching voices singing along.
Buffets sound like slamming tabletops,
smell like brewing tea and sugar packets.
Hot tubs are too hot or too cold,
too close or not close enough.
Doors held open remind me some people are good,
hand on back reminds me that most people are not.
Hotel rooms taste like milkshakes and bellyaches,
stacks of Oreos and the sinking feeling of time to go.

There is nowhere I can go and nothing I can do
that won't feel like another time or another place.
I have lived a thousand lifetimes
and I forget that there was a time
in which there was anything
that didn't feel like a memory.

the things that matter

I've found that there are people I can cry to
while lost on a college campus or
in a cold hotel room, an empty classroom,
a crowded subway.
And they will still be there for me as they were
when I was smiling and positive and bubbly.
I used to think I could only be loved
(only deserved love)
when sadness wasn't etched onto my face,
when my mouth wasn't creased into a frown.

I've learned that my acceptance letters
are just as significant as my failures-
there are people that stuck by me through both.
I've given lingering hugs when I knew
that I wouldn't see that person for a while,
struggling to say,
"I will miss you more than anything."
But not saying it,
because I didn't want to be the only one
who cared so much.
I tackled that same person with a giant bear hug
the next time I saw them-
finally finding the strength to say-
"I missed you more than anything."

These are the things that matter.
Not only when I am alone,
or feeling isolated.
This is what matters
when I'm living in these moments-
looking around and thinking-
'I don't want this to end.'
It is to wish that moments would last forever
on every shooting star,
cake candle, and dandelion blown to the wind.

I know that I am not entitled to anything,
but how lucky am I to spend time
with people who feel like home.

I am not just now realizing how important
these moments are because I am alone,
or wishing for them back because I *deserve* them.

I always knew that they were temporary.

But things that are temporary
are often the most beautiful.

growing into myself

I'm made of sunshine,
letting it rest in my bones.
laden with light, bursting with warmth.
I'm letting the mornings come in a blaze of light.
The days don't feel like a chore.
Like picking the weeds or
putting on sunscreen. It's a celebration-
planting a garden, staring up at the sun.
Soaking it up. Not just the sun, but this life.
I hold it in my cupped hands like a lightning bug,
and there's not one part of me
that wants to disappear.
Not one part of me that wants anything
but to burn bright.

I open my hands and let the firefly flit into the night.
I can't hold the day in my hands, my joy in my hands-
it fills the whole sky. It lives in the sun,
floats alongside the clouds.
This life feels like something beautiful
and I'm starting to fall in love with it.
I'm starting to see myself in the sun,
I'm calling the sunshine mine-
this can only be a good thing.

what a tragedy

I like to become a stranger in my own home,
pretend I don't know where every street sign leads.
Wander like I haven't biked through every park,
comment on the weather like it isn't always the same.
This is how I relearn what I already know.

When I go anywhere new,
I marvel at everything
like it holds some sort of magic.
I look at the people wandering their hometown
and think what a tragedy
that they have grown used to
this place they call home.
They don't see the glowing neon lights
of the secondhand record shop
as anything but tacky.
The local diner is boring,
the town is a temporary stage-
'I can't wait to get away.'

What a tragedy
that we get used to the beauty around us,
as if seeing it everyday
takes away its wonder.

When I started viewing new places and
the people who lived there in this way-
I changed the way I thought of my own home.
I rediscovered the beauty I had become immune to.

I think the biggest tragedy of all
is that we so often fail
to see what's right in front of us.

storm warning

My mind gives me a storm warning;
alarms blaring and colors flashing.
Tropical storm building into a hurricane, but
all I can do is sit and watch.
I build up blockades, put up my shutters,
but it's never enough, never enough.

The wreckage is astounding.
I am the devastation and I am left devastated.
I am the storm and the aftermath.
Ruthless in tearing myself down,
determined in building myself back up.

Some days I don't hide inside, I don't bunker down.
Some days I know the storm is coming
and I read outside, tilt my head towards the sun
before it disappears.
When the sky darkens, when the clouds form,
I let the rain fall. It soaks through my clothes-
teeth clatter, settle in my bones.
I laugh, shake my fist at the sky.

And I know this poem is
a metaphor to say I can't feel at home in wreckage-
but what happens when you welcome the wreckage?
When you become it?

I don't know that I've changed at all
if I still hide from the wreckage or embody it,
but nothing in between.

Growth is not just the sunflowers blooming
behind houses, in fields. Growth is also
the weeds in between the rows of fruits,
it's the slow suffocation: It is all part of the garden.
Growth is learning to accept both.

My mind might feel like a disaster zone,
but it is home. I am home.
I am coming back to myself.

in conclusion

I've been taught to always say 'in conclusion'
once I reach the end.
I've never been good at endings,
goodbyes and farewells.
Instead, I say things like,
'Maybe it's over,'
'Almost done.'

I can't start a story without thinking
about the ending.
It is obvious in every word, sentence, page.
I'm left clinging to something that no longer is.
I don't know when my life
became a structured essay:
three points and a thesis.
When my endings became a jumble of,
'See you later' and 'Catch you on the flip side,'
personal anecdote turned sob story.

So, this is my best attempt.

In conclusion,
my growth does not need a conclusion.
It does not end
and cannot be measured within three paragraphs.
I am a complete work in progress
and I am learning how to love it.

Acknowledgements

This book wouldn't have been possible without the endless love and support from so many people. First- to my mom, dad, and brother Adam- thank you for always believing in me and my dreams. You mean everything to me.

To Amira, Grace, Kristina, Marissa, Natalie, Alexis, and Avani; thank you for encouraging me since the first poems, the first drafts. Thank you for sharing in my joy and excitement through every step of the process. I would be lost without such incredible friends.

To all my family and friends that have been here not only since the start of this collection, but for my whole life- thank you for joining me in this chapter.

A huge thank you to my readers! Whether you know me in real life or found my poetry on Instagram; it means the world to me that you're here. I'm so thankful to the poetry community on Instagram for how welcome you all have made me feel, for reading everything I write and being so supportive of it. Big thank you especially to my beta reader Lydia Redwine and copy editor Caitlin Conlon.

Finally, my Abuelita, to whom this book is dedicated. I love and miss you more than I can describe.

About the Author

A complete work in progress is Nia Mahmud's debut poetry collection, she self-published it at the age of seventeen. Nia has always loved reading and writing, her biggest dream growing up was to one day publish a book. With this book that dream is a reality! When she's not writing poetry, you can find her listening to Taylor Swift, hanging out with friends and family, or watching Netflix. Nia is a poet, storyteller, and essayist. Her poetry and essays have been published in several magazines. You can find her on Instagram @nia.m.writer to see more of her writing.

Made in the USA
Columbia, SC
05 November 2021

48392647R00074